Call of the Night

〈16〉

KOTOYAMA

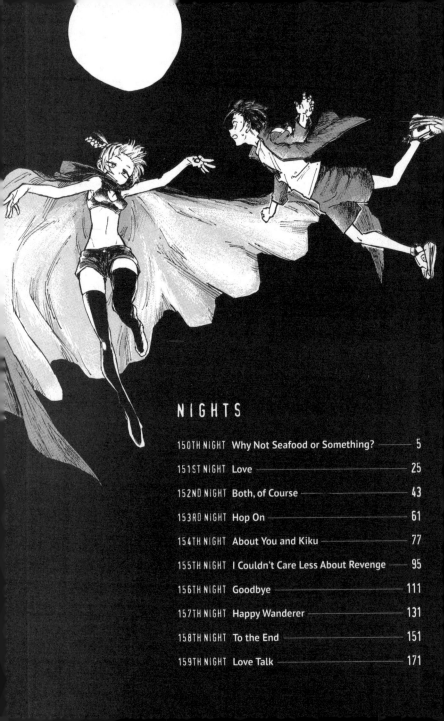

NIGHTS

150TH NIGHT Why Not Seafood or Something? ——— 5

151ST NIGHT Love ——— 25

152ND NIGHT Both, of Course ——— 43

153RD NIGHT Hop On ——— 61

154TH NIGHT About You and Kiku ——— 77

155TH NIGHT I Couldn't Care Less About Revenge ——— 95

156TH NIGHT Goodbye ——— 111

157TH NIGHT Happy Wanderer ——— 131

158TH NIGHT To the End ——— 151

159TH NIGHT Love Talk ——— 171

NIGHT 150: WHY NOT SEAFOOD OR SOMETHING?

NIGHT 150:
WHY NOT SEAFOOD OR SOMETHING?

I WONDER IF THEY'VE MADE UP YET.

HMM...

THE POWER OF FRIENDSHIP TRIUMPHS! HA HA...

I GUESS ALL'S WELL THAT ENDS WELL.

TMP TMP TMP

MAHIRU SEEMED SO GLAD TO SEE HIM.

HELLO, AKIRA. WHAT BRINGS YOU HERE?

MS. DETEC-TIVE!

TMP TMP

OH!

HUH?

OKAY, OKAY!

THIS ISN'T MY FAULT!

WHAT KIND OF IDIOT TRIES TO RESOLVE A CONFLICT BY CHASING SOMEONE AROUND WITH A SWORD?

HOW WAS I SUPPOSED TO KNOW THAT WOULD HAPPEN?!

MAHIRU MAY RUN FROM YAMORI...

...BUT HE CAN'T ESCAPE THIS CITY.

HUH? WHY NOT?

WELL...

ONE THING'S FOR SURE.

ZZT

...HE WAS COMPLETELY BAFFLED BY THE BUS TIMETABLE.

WHEN I FOUND MAHIRU...

HE WAS BABBLING ABOUT US FIGHTING.

WHAT WAS THAT ALL ABOUT?

BUT SOMETHING WAS OFF. *HE* WAS OFF.

AT FIRST I THOUGHT IT WAS REVENGE.

Heh heh heh heh

...

HE WAS JUST HIS NORMAL SELF.

IF HE WANTED TO BEAT THE CRAP OUT OF ME, WHY DIDN'T HE TURN INTO A "HALF VAMPIRE" OR WHATEVER?

BESIDES...

WE BATTLE EACH OTHER... AND THEN WHAT?

WAS HE TRYING TO INSTIGATE SOME KIND OF *PLAY-GROUND FIGHT*?

YOU'VE HELPED ME...

THANKS, KO.

KO...

...

...COME TO A DECISION.

WHAT?! THEN WHY'D YOU LET ME WASTE ALL THIS TIME LOOKING FOR HIM?!

DON'T WORRY, KO. I KNOW WHERE WE CAN FIND HIM.

WHAA

BECAUSE YOU WERE ROMPING IN THE FLUSH OF YOUTH.

GLOOOOOM

...

LOST HIM, HUH?

YOU REALLY ARE USELESS IN YOUR HUMAN FORM.

HE WANTS TO VISIT A SPOT THAT'S MEMORABLE TO HIM.

YOU TOLD ME YOU LOOKED THROUGH MAHIRU'S FAMILY PHOTO ALBUM WHEN YOU WENT TO HIS HOUSE.

!

YOU DON'T NEED ME TO TELL YOU. YOU'RE THE ONE WHO TIPPED ME OFF.

FINE, WHATEVER. WHERE'S HE HEADED?

WE'LL HEAD DOWN THERE TONIGHT.

!!

SH WA AA

THE VIEW IS SPECTAC-ULAR.

YOU'LL LIKE IT.

UM...

DINNER'S ON ME.

MEAN-WHILE, ARE YOU TWO HUNGRY?

THIS IS GOOD STUFF.

SIGH... KIDS TODAY.

WE'RE IN HOKKAIDO. WHY NOT SEAFOOD OR SOME-THING?

YOU PICKED A FAST-FOOD CHAIN YOU COULD'VE GONE TO BACK HOME.

Call of the Night

Call of the Night

NIGHT 151: LOVE

NIGHT 151: LOVE

MAHIRU...

NO. THE TRUTH IS, I'VE NEVER FELT THIS WAY BEFORE.

A FEELING I'D LONG FORGOTTEN.

SO THIS IS LOVE.

YUP.

I'M IN LOVE.

THAT MAKES THIS MY FIRST LOVE.

34

HE LIED TO ME!

HE HELD ON TO THIS! HE HID IT FROM ME!

KRRRK

I TOLD HIM TO DESTROY EVERYTHING FROM HIS OLD LIFE!

WHY? WHY? WHY?! I THOUGHT HE THREW THIS AWAY!!

WHY...?

HFF HFF

WHY?!

IT'S ON.

...

THE POWER...

DID HE FORGET IT? HOW COME?

BUT IF HE WAS *HIDING* IT, WHY LEAVE IT HERE?

IF YOU KNOW, DO IT! OTHERWISE, MAMA GET MAD!

I KNOW, I KNOW, BUT...

C'MON! YOU STILL HAVEN'T TALKED TO HIM? WOMAN UP AND SAY THE WORDS!

HEY, IS KO IN?

SO... MANY... GIRLS...

HE'S NOT HERE? WHERE'D HE GO?

WE MET HER ON THE TRAIN.

WHO'S SHE?

CAN'T LET MY GUARD DOWN! HAVE TO BE READY TO GO HALF VAMP AT ANY SECOND!

IS THAT A JOKE?

...YOU'D ACTUALLY *OBEY* ME.

SURE, BUT I DIDN'T THINK...

...

UM, YOU *TOLD* ME TO COME ALONE.

WELL, THANK YOU.

HERE COME THE FANGS...

I SUMMONED YOU HERE BECAUSE YOU'RE CLOSE TO MAHIRU.

SHF

...?

WHY AM I NOT ENOUGH TO SATISFY HIM?!

WHAT IS MAHIRU THINKING? I CAN'T FIGURE IT OUT!

DOESN'T HE LIKE ME ANYMORE? IS HE BORED WITH ME?

UH... WHAT?

NIGHT 152: BOTH, OF COURSE

I CAN'T FIGURE OUT WHAT MAHIRU'S THINKING!

DOESN'T HE LIKE ME ANYMORE? IS HE BORED WITH ME?

UM...

WHAT THE HELL IS SHE TALKING ABOUT?!

WHY AM I NOT ENOUGH TO SATISFY HIM?!

NIGHT 152:

BOTH, OF COURSE

WHAT
IS...

HOW COME
SHE'S
FREAKING
OUT ALL
OF A
SUDDEN?

AND
WHAT'S
SHE
SAYING
ABOUT
MAHIRU?!

...
GOING
ON?

...HE DOESN'T LIKE YOU ANYMORE?

DID MAHIRU SAY...

NOT IN WORDS?

NO. NOT IN SO MANY WORDS...

WAIT!

!

DON'T RAISE YOUR VOICE! IT'S STRESSING ME OUT!

THEN WHAT'S THE PROBLEM?

HUH ?!

LISTEN!

YOU'RE THE ONLY PERSON I CAN TALK TO ABOUT THIS.

AT ITS HEART, IT'S ABOUT...

TRUE LOVE.

WHAT DO YOU THINK LOVE IS?

...*SELF-SACRIFICE,* RIGHT?

...THE TRUER YOUR LOVE IS.

THE MORE YOU GIVE UP FOR YOUR LOVED ONE...

DON'T LOOK AT ME LIKE I'M CRAZY!

IF YOU HAVE LOVE, YOU DON'T NEED ANYTHING ELSE! THAT'S HOW IT WORKS!

HOW DARE YOU SAY THAT?!

THAT'S THE STUPIDEST THING I'VE EVER HEARD!

WELL...

I NEED *ACTIONS*.

BUT WORDS AREN'T ENOUGH.

FINE. WHATEVER. TELL THAT TO *MAHIRU* THEN!

HIS *FRIENDS*!!

MAHIRU GAVE UP *EVERYTHING* FOR YOU! HIS LIFE! HIS FAMILY!

...

I HOPE SOMEDAY YOU GET TO FEEL THAT TOO.

THE WORLD FLOODED WITH BEAUTY, AND I FINALLY KNEW HAPPINESS.

WE WERE HAVING AN ORDINARY CONVERSATION, AND OUT OF THE BLUE, I THOUGHT, "I LOVE HIM."

KNOW WHAT? I FINALLY FELL IN LOVE WITH HIM. FOR REAL.

HE PROMISED HE WOULD DESTROY IT.

 THIS IS...

SHF

...HIS PHONE.

 ....!

 BUT HE *LIED.*

SHUP

MAYBE IT'S JUST A MISUNDERSTANDING.

UM... WHY DON'T YOU ASK *HIM*?

WHY WOULD HE LIE TO ME?!

SWOO

 HE SAID HE GOT RID OF *EVERYTHING.*

I CAN'T TELL THE GUY I LOVE THAT I SNOOPED IN HIS PHONE!

HOW *CAN* I?

WHAT IS MAHIRU TO YOU?

THAT'S WHY I WANTED TO TALK TO YOU.

IF HE FINDS OUT, HE'LL HATE ME.

RIGHT. THAT IS KINDA SKEEVY.

CONGRATS ON DIS-COVERING BASIC ETHICS, I GUESS...

MY *FRIEND.*

GIVEN THE CHOICE BETWEEN YOUR LOVER OR YOUR FRIEND, WHO WOULD YOU CHOOSE? YOUR LOVER, RIGHT?

SO IF I HAVE TO SACRIFICE FOR MY LOVER...

RIGHT. UNFORTUNATELY, I DON'T HAVE MUCH LEFT TO GIVE UP.

IF I HAVE TO CHOOSE SOMETHING... IT WOULD BE...

YOU MADE HIM SACRIFICE JUST ABOUT EVERYTHING.

BY THE WAY, WHAT HAVE *YOU* GIVEN UP FOR *HIM*?

HOW CAN YOU MATCH THAT?

BOTH, OF COURSE.

YOU DON'T HAVE TO CHOOSE.

I THOUGHT KIKU HOSHIMI WAS BAD NEWS.

...GET MAHIRU BACK BY PROVING THAT HE WAS BEING LED ON.

I THOUGHT I COULD...

...FROM THE START, SHE'S NEVER REALLY *LIED*. SHE ONLY HID HER VAMPIRE IDENTITY BECAUSE SHE WAS AFRAID OF SCARING MAHIRU AWAY.

BUT COME TO THINK OF IT...

...BUT THE WHOLE TIME, SHE WAS JUST TRYING TO FIGURE OUT LOVE.

OKAY, KIKU *HAS* RUINED A LOT OF LIVES AND MADE A LOT OF CONFUSED VAMPIRES...

SHE'S A LOT LIKE...

IT'S *MY* FAULT HE FOUND OUT.

...ME.

SHAK

KIKU...

I USE THEM TO TURN INTO A HALF VAMPIRE.

KRRRR

WHAT ARE THOSE?

ALL I WANT IS TO PATCH THINGS UP WITH MY FRIEND.

KRRRRR

I WON'T SAY YOU HAVEN'T DONE SOME CRAPPY THINGS, BUT...

I THINK I'VE MISJUDGED YOU TILL NOW.

I WANT TO TALK TO HIM AS A HUMAN BEING.

LET'S GO TALK TO MAHIRU TOGETHER—YOU AND ME.

I'M NOT GOING TO TRY TO BREAK YOU TWO UP ANYMORE.

Call of the Night

Call of the Night

NIGHT 153: **HOP ON**

DID I IMAGINE THAT FANGY SMIRK?

KIKU TOLD ME TO FOLLOW HER. SO HERE WE ARE, STROLLING THROUGH THE NIGHT TOGETHER.

BUT I STILL HAVE ONE QUESTION...

WELL, IT WORKED. SHE'S TAKING ME TO SEE MAHIRU.

SHF

SHF

...BUT MAYBE IT WASN'T THE BRIGHTEST IDEA TO SMASH ALL MY PIERCERS.

I WANTED HER TO TRUST ME...

...I JUMPED TO THE CONCLUSION THAT YOU WERE TRYING TO KILL MAHIRU.

WHEN I HEARD THAT STORY...

IF A VAMPIRE FEEDS FROM SOMEONE THEY LOVE...

...ACCORDING TO LEGEND, THAT PERSON WILL DIE.

WHAT?

UM, KIKU?

MAY I ASK YOU SOME-THING?

...?

OH, YES.

HEY, JUST SO YOU KNOW, I'VE NEVER LIED TO MAHIRU.

...

THANKS. THAT'S GOOD TO HEAR.

HE CONSENTED TO EVERYTHING.

THIS SPOT WILL DO.

WHAT...

?

SWIP

BETTER TO KILL YOU WHILE YOU'RE MORTAL.

BLOODSHED TENDS TO TRIGGER THE VAMPIRE IN YOU, RIGHT?

MOST BATTLES BETWEEN VAMPIRES END IN A DRAW.

SUCH A WASTE OF TIME.

IT WOULD HAVE BEEN TOO MUCH TROUBLE FOR ME TO SUBDUE YOU IN YOUR VAMPIRIC FORM.

HEY.

NIGHT 154:

ABOUT YOU AND KIKU

HARUKA
...?

...

YOU WANNA SEE YOUR FRIEND OR NOT?

!

KO! HOP ON ALREADY!

LONG TIME NO SEE.

YEAH!

OH!

DASH

Y-YOU'RE NOT...

...GOING ANY-WHERE!

SPLOSH

!

YOUR TURN.

ABOUT TIME.

KLAK

THANKS, KO.

KLAK

86

WE'RE JUST HERE AS REFEREES...

SPLOSH

SPLOSH

PHEW...

BAM

...SO THIS MORTAL CAN TALK TO YOU ON AN EQUAL FOOTING.

HA HA... I SEE...

I'M DOING IT AS A FAVOR TO NAZUNA.

PIPPI ASKED ME TO!

THANKS.

HEH... TWO FOOLS IN LOVE.

NOPE, *I* DID. I GOT KO TO TELL ME ABOUT YOUR LITTLE MEETUP.

AND THAT BOY BEGGED *ME* TO BE HONEST.

SO THIS WAS A TRAP *FROM THE START.*

HE PLAYED *DIRTY!*

SPLASH

TP TP

HER WOUND IS TAKING A WHILE TO HEAL...

SIIIGH...

DOESN'T MATTER WHO IT WAS.

MAKE IT SNAPPY, WILL YOU?

WHAT DO YOU WANT TO TALK ABOUT?

WELL, WHAT IS IT?

HEY...

WHAAAT?! SORRY! IT'S JUST... TALKING ABOUT TH-TH-THIS...

YOU'RE EMBARRASSED, AREN'T YOU?

PHEEEW...

I SAID, SORRY! GIMME A SEC!

GET TO THE CHIT-CHAT!

'KAY.
SO.

WHAT'S
IT LIKE
FALLING
IN LOVE
WITH A
VAMPIRE?

TELL
ME
ABOUT...

...YOU
AND
KIKU.

Call of the Night

Call of the *Night*

NIGHT 155:

I COULDN'T CARE LESS ABOUT REVENGE

I TOLD YOU TO MAKE THIS SNAPPY.

...

YOU COULD SAY THAT.

IS THERE SOMETHING YOU WANT FROM ME?

WELL?

I KNOW YOU'VE BEEN STALKING US.

YOU'RE A DETECTIVE, RIGHT?

AND?

OH?

I'VE BEEN AFTER YOU FOR TEN LONG YEARS.

SEE...

I HAVE A QUESTION.

IS THAT TRUE?

AS LONG AS SHE'S GROOMING KO'S FRIEND, SHE WON'T FEED ON ANYONE ELSE.

AZAMI SAID...

...KIKU'S THE TYPE OF VAMPIRE WHO ONLY TARGETS ONE HUMAN AT A TIME.

I'M NOT THE KIND TO DWELL ON OLD ROMANCES...

...BUT THERE HAVE BEEN A *FEW* MEMORABLE ONES.

HOW MANY OF THE PEOPLE YOU'VE TURNED DO YOU REMEMBER?

...

NOT SURE. WHAT ABOUT HIM?

WHAT ABOUT A MAN NAMED MICHIHISA KANO?

GET TO THE POINT.

AND...?

JUST ABOUT TEN YEARS AGO.

YOU TURNED HIM.

RECENTLY, I TRACKED HIM DOWN.

I KILLED HIM.

THAT'S NOT YOUR USUAL M.O., IS IT?

...THE *ONLY* PERSON YOU TURNED AROUND THAT TIME.

BUT HE WASN'T...

...

I SEE.

...

SO HERE'S MY QUESTION.

103

I TAKE IT MY FATHER IS ONE OF THE MEMORABLE ONES.

...

HMPH...

PHEEEW!!

OH...

...

BUT I COULDN'T LEAVE IT AT THAT.

OF COURSE, I BLAMED MY DAD FOR BETRAYING HIS FAMILY.

FOR SO LONG I'VE WANTED...

FOR THE PAST DECADE, MY ONLY THOUGHT WAS TO SLAY YOU.

...TO KILL YOU.

BUT NOW...

HEY, KYOKO.

HI, NAZUNA.

SHUP

I FINISHED THE BOOK YOU LOANED ME.

THE FIRST HALF WAS OKAY, BUT THE ENDING KINDA SUCKED.

EH...

HOW'D YOU LIKE IT?

OH, YEAH?

SO THEY NEVER GET THEIR REVENGE! JUSTICE ISN'T SERVED!

THE WHOLE STORY JUST FIZZLES OUT...

WELL, YEAH.

BUT THE DETECTIVE FIGURES THAT OUT AND PREVENTS IT.

I MEAN, THE BAD GUY IS BASICALLY OBSESSED WITH REVENGE, RIGHT?

...?

I THINK THAT'S THE THEME OF THE NOVEL.

KRRRK...

THE POINT OF REVENGE IS REVENGE ITSELF.

PEOPLE DON'T SEEK REVENGE TO *GAIN* SOMETHING.

BUT YOU HAVE TO PUT YOURSELF IN THE OTHER PERSON'S SHOES.

OF COURSE, THAT'S EASY TO SAY IF YOU'RE NOT THE INJURED PARTY.

LOGICALLY, REVENGE IS POINTLESS.

IN THE END, THE DETECTIVE SAYS...

AT LEAST, NOT IN A MYSTERY NOVEL.

BUT "TA-DA! YOU GOT YOUR REVENGE!" WOULDN'T BE A HAPPY ENDING.

happy end

...*"I SOLVED THE CASE. THAT'S ALL."*

"I COULDN'T CARE LESS..."

"...ABOUT REVENGE."

NIGHT 156:

GOODBYE

114

115

WHY COULDN'T SHE DODGE THAT?

...

WE AGREED NOT TO KILL KIKU.

DID YOU CHANGE YOUR MIND?

WHAT ARE YOU DOING?!

DETECTIVE LADY!

ARE YOU SATISFIED NOW?

I WAS JUST *PISSED OFF*, THAT'S ALL.

...

ALL THESE CENTURIES OF UNDEAD EXISTENCE, YOU'VE BEEN FRUSTRATED.

YOU'RE NO HAPPIER THAN I AM.

YOU WANT TO BE *MORTAL*, DON'T YOU?

HEY, KIKU. WHAT WOULD SATISFY *YOU*?

I DON'T KNOW IF *ANYTHING* COULD SATISFY ME.

118

119

... ENOUGH FOR YOU?

... WASN'T HE...

NO ONE IS AS SURPRISED AS SHE IS.

IT JUST POPPED OUT OF HER MOUTH.

THIS IS NOT THE QUESTION SHE INTENDED TO ASK.

124

SWIp

...

...

SHUP

TMP

KIKU!

TMP

TMP

HEY...

HEY, KYOKO...

STOP!

DETECTIVE LADY! SHE'S LEAVING!! ARE YOU JUST GONNA LET HER GO?

FP

127

GOOD-BYE...

Call of the Night

Call of the Night

NIGHT 157:

HAPPY
WANDERER

WE CAN TALK UNTIL SHE SHOWS UP.

YEAH, I KNOW.

...WAITING FOR KIKU.

UM. I'M...

...

YOU'RE KO'S FRIEND.

ME TOO. SO LET'S GET TO KNOW EACH OTHER.

LOOK, I DON'T GIVE A CRAP ABOUT YOUR TRYING-TO-GET-TURNED DRAMA.

MAHIRU?

!

YEAH, THANKS.

WANT ME TO DELIVER THAT ORDER?

WHAT'S UP, DAD?

WELL, SON...

YOU'VE GOT SCHOOL. AND THERE'S YOUR MOM TO WORRY ABOUT...

...BUT ARE YOU SURE IT'S NOT TOO MUCH FOR YOU?

IT'S NOT THAT I DON'T APPRECIATE YOUR HELPING OUT AROUND THE SHOP...

FLOWERS

IF YOU'RE WORRIED ABOUT HER, WHY DON'T *YOU* LOOK AFTER HER?

MUTTER

JACKASS.

SWIP

THAT IS... ER...

THE FLOWER SHOP COULD GO BUST TOO, FOR ALL I CARED.

I USED TO WISH THE PLACE WOULD JUST DISAPPEAR.

SPINN

BEING AT HOME WAS MISERABLE.

BUT...

I DIDN'T REALLY WANT TO HELP OUT WITH THE FAMILY BUSINESS.

138

ALL I COULD THINK WAS...

..."WOW, LOOK AT *HER*."

ARE YOU FROM THE FLORIST?

THEY'RE SO PRETTY!

YEAH, PRETTY...

AND THIS IS FOR YOU.

...THE HELL AM I DOING? AM I TRYING TO *HIT* ON HER?!

ARRGH! KILL ME NOW! SHE'LL THINK I'M SOME CRINGEY KID!

W-WHAT...

THANKS.

I NEVER DO STUFF LIKE THIS.

SHE'S SO GROWN-UP.

I....

DOES IT SYMBOLIZE ANYTHING?

What's the name of this flower?

AND COOL.

I think it's Hardenbergia.

I WAS JUST TOO NERVOUS TO TELL HER.

THE THING IS, I HADN'T FORGOTTEN.

I FORGET.

AWW!

THAT BLOOM IS CALLED "THE HAPPY WANDERER."

NEXT TIME WE SEE EACH OTHER, YOU CAN TELL ME.

IN THE LANGUAGE OF FLOWERS, IT MEANS "FATEFUL ENCOUNTER."

KRRK

...A NEXT TIME?

THERE'S GONNA BE...

SHFF

THERE'S...

SHFF

SHFF

SHFF

...GONNA BE A NEXT TIME!

SHFF

SHFF

SHFF

SHFF

SHFF

WHAT DOES SHE LIKE? I WANT TO KNOW EVERYTHING ABOUT HER!

WHERE'S SHE FROM? IS SHE LOCAL?

I WONDER HOW OLD SHE IS. I HEAR YOU'RE NOT SUPPOSED TO ASK A WOMAN HER AGE.

AS IT TURNED OUT, SHE WAS UNDEAD.

WELL...

Yay!

IN FACT, I BECAME EVEN *MORE* INFATUATED.

BUT THAT DIDN'T CHANGE MY FEELINGS FOR HER.

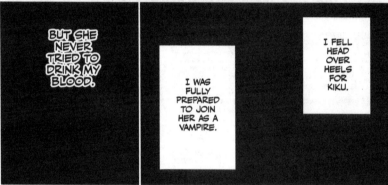

BUT SHE NEVER TRIED TO DRINK MY BLOOD.

I WAS FULLY PREPARED TO JOIN HER AS A VAMPIRE.

I FELL HEAD OVER HEELS FOR KIKU.

BUT...

ONE DAY...

MAHIRU?

I WAS FINE WITH THAT...

...AS LONG AS WE GOT TO HANG OUT.

146

DIE?! WHY WOULD YOU SAY THAT?!

OH...

WHA... WHAT?!

YES, MAHIRU?

HUH?

SO, MAHIRU...

MY FEEDING CYCLE GETS SHORTER YEAR BY YEAR.

I CAN JUST SENSE IT.

...?

MY DREAM...

148

Call of the Night

Call of the Night

HALLOWEEN.

IT WAS OCTOBER 31.

...TO A *HOTEL*.

KIKU HAD INVITED ME...

...I WAS PRETTY EXCITED!

TO TELL YOU THE TRUTH...

I WONDER WHAT SHE'S GOING TO WEAR. WHATEVER IT IS, I BET SHE'LL LOOK SUUUUUPER HOT!

DOES THIS MEAN I GET TO SEE HER IN COSTUME?

152

NIGHT 158:
TO THE END

WHAT
ARE
YOU...

WHY
WOULD
I DO
THAT?!

...
SAYING?

WHY ?!

MAHIR–

I...I MEAN...

IT'S...

YOU'RE GONNA DIE? YOU WANT ME TO KILL YOU?

WHAT THE HELL ARE YOU TALKING ABOUT?!

MAHIRU...

...HALLO-WEEN.

159

SO THAT'S WHY SHE WON'T FEED FROM ME.

...SHE'S ABLE TO DIE.

SHE WON'T TAKE ME UNTIL...

SO...

...KO...

KO? I'VE DECIDED.

I'M GOING TO BECOME A VAMPIRE TOO.

IF KIKU TURNED ME, I'D HAVE SOMEONE TO BE WITH FOREVER!

I COULD LEAVE MY MISERABLE HOME LIFE AND MOVE IN WITH HER.

...I WAS SURPRISED, OF COURSE, BUT ALSO EXCITED.

WHEN I FOUND OUT KIKU WAS A VAMPIRE...

I'D FINALLY BEAT YOU, KO.

AND...

YOU'RE SO LUCKY...

PRETTY CHILDISH, HUH?

...TO FALL IN LOVE. AND ONCE YOU DO, IT NEVER HAS TO END.

SO LUCKY.

YOU GET TO TAKE YOUR SWEET TIME...

NO MATTER HOW MUCH I WANT IT, THERE'S NO WAY I CAN BE WITH KIKU FOREVER.

DAMN YOU.

...KILL HER.

AFTER ALL, THAT DETECTIVE LADY IS OUT TO...

BUT KIKU WANTS *ME* TO BE THE ONE TO DO IT.

WHAT-EVER I DO...

WHETHER OR NOT SHE FALLS FOR ME...

...KIKU IS GOING TO DIE ONE WAY OR ANOTHER.

SO...

RICH & NATURAL

¥130

COLD

MAHIRU!!

HUH?

IT'S MORNING ALREADY ...?

KIKU ...

ARE YOU ALL RIGHT? DID ANYONE GIVE YOU A HARD TIME?

I WAS WORRIED SICK!

WHERE HAVE YOU BEEN?

IT'S *MORNING!!* YOU CAN'T BE OUTSIDE!!

!

WHAT ARE YOU DOING HERE?!

I GOT WORRIED...

BUT...

THAT'S RIGHT.

OH...

FEELING BETTER NOW?

YEAH. SORRY TO WORRY YOU.

KIKU...

KIKU!!

AH...

Call of the Night

Call of the Night

THAT'S WHY I'M GOING TO KILL KIKU.

UH... HUH.

...

NIGHT 159:

LOVE TALK

PROBABLY MORE THAN I'VE THOUGHT ABOUT BECOMING A VAMPIRE.

IT'S NOT LIKE I *WANT* TO.

BUT I'VE THOUGHT IT OVER VERY CAREFULLY.

YEAH.

YOU'RE GONNA GO THROUGH WITH THAT TOO, THEN.

YOU'LL BE TURNED, BUT SHE'LL BE DEAD. AND YOU'LL JUST, LIKE, WHAT...? GO ON WITH YOUR UNDEAD LIFE?

I DON'T GET IT. HOW CAN YOU BE COOL WITH THAT?

THAT'S GONNA REALLY SUCK.

HMMMMM...

SKRCH SKRCH

LIKE I SAID, WHETHER OR NOT I'M THE ONE TO DO IT, SHE'S GOING TO DIE.

BUT KIKU IS *EVERY-THING* TO ME.

WE DON'T HAVE A LOT OF TIME LEFT TOGETHER...

WHEN YOU PUT IT THAT WAY IT SOUNDS HARSH...

WELL ...

...

...UNLIKE *YOU* TWO.

HOW COME YOU'RE SO READY TO BELIEVE WHATEVER SHE SAYS?

YOU DON'T HAVE PROOF THAT ANYTHING SHE'S TOLD YOU IS TRUE.

Y'KNOW ...

I LOVE HER, SO I BELIEVE HER.

BECAUSE I LOVE HER.

EITHER WAY, I DON'T CARE.

MAYBE SHE'S LYING. MAYBE SHE'S BEING AS HONEST AS SHE CAN BE.

IF THAT'S TRUE...

KIKU MEANS THE WORLD TO ME.

...HOW CAN YOU BE OKAY WITH LOSING HER FOREVER?

OKAY, OKAY.

IT'S *BECAUSE* I LOVE HER...

I MEAN, YOU'LL HAVE WON YOUR RACE WITH HIM, RIGHT?

YOU'VE *GOTTA* MAKE UP WITH KO AFTER THAT.

BUT THAT MEANS TONIGHT'S THE NIGHT YOU BECOME A VAMP.

YEAH, WELL...

I HAVEN'T TALKED TO HIM SINCE... YOU KNOW...

WELL...

WHERE'D *THAT* COME FROM?

I KNOW I NEED TO APOLO-GIZE...

UM... SORRY ABOUT THAT. I GUESS I HAVEN'T BEEN MYSELF LATELY.

ARGH!!

HE WAS SUPER-DUPER DEPRESSED ABOUT YOU HATING HIM.

SOME-
TIMES HE
ACTS LIKE
A BRATTY
KID...

HA
HA
...

...BUT
OTHER
TIMES
HE'S THIS
TAKE-
CHARGE
DUDE.

KO'S
WEIRD.

!

SWIP

THAT'S KO,
ALL RIGHT!

YEAH. HA HA...

WHERE YA HEADED? I'LL GIVE YOU A LIFT.

THIS ROAD IS DANGEROUS AT NIGHT.

THANK YOU. I REALLY APPRECIATE IT.

NO PROBLEM.

GOING OUT TO THE CAPE, HUH?

WHAT A STROKE OF LUCK! BUT...HOW DO I TALK TO A HUMAN WOMAN? I NEVER KNOW WHAT TO SAY TO THEM.

AT LEAST SHE DIDN'T ASK ABOUT MY FACE.

WHY D'YOU WANNA GO THERE?

NOT MUCH TO SEE IN THE DARK.

HOPE YOU'RE NOT PLANNING TO, Y'KNOW...*OFF* YOURSELF.

I'M MEETING THE MAN I LOVE. THAT'S ALL.

HA HA!

OHHH, SO THAT'S IT!

THESE LONG HAULS GET AWFUL BORING.

OKAY, GO AHEAD AND BRAG ABOUT YOUR BOYFRIEND.

TO BE CONTINUED...

Afterword

Kotoyama here. It's volume 16 already. I can't believe it! When I was working on these chapters, I kept thinking, "They're so looooooooong!" I read over the story arc, and I still think it was a tad long. This is an area I could improve on. I need to reflect on that.

I don't like to specify where this story takes place exactly. I've been using actual locations as models for backgrounds, but lately I've become worried that this might cause problems for the locals...although I haven't heard of any concerns so far. Apparently, people are easily identifying the real-life sources for my locations. Basically, what I'm trying to say is that it's my fault for drawing them in such a way that they're so identifiable. I think I need to be more careful in the future. But I'll continue to work hard to create attractive settings for the story.

Well then, see you in volume 17. Thank you for reading!

Kotoyama

My writer's callus hurts all the time. It stopped for a little while, and I thought I'd won, but it's starting to hurt again. What's up with this guy?

— KOTOYAMA

KOTOYAMA

In 2013, Kotoyama won the Shonen Sunday Manga College Award for *Azuma*. From 2014 to 2018, Kotoyama's title *Dagashi Kashi* ran in *Shonen Sunday* magazine. *Call of the Night* has been published in *Shonen Sunday* since 2019.

Call of the Night

⟨16⟩

SHONEN SUNDAY EDITION

Story and Art by
KOTOYAMA

Translation – JUNKO GODA
English Adaptation – SHAENON K. GARRITY
Touch-Up Art & Lettering – ANNALIESE "ACE" CHRISTMAN
Cover & Interior Design – PAUL PADURARIU
Editor – ANNETTE ROMAN

YOFUKASHI NO UTA Vol. 16
by KOTOYAMA
© 2019 KOTOYAMA
All rights reserved.
Original Japanese edition published by SHOGAKUKAN.
English translation rights in the United States of America, Canada, the United Kingdom,
Ireland, Australia and New Zealand arranged with SHOGAKUKAN.

Original Cover Design – Yasuhisa KAWATANI

Printed in the U.S.A.

Published by VIZ Media, LLC
P.O. Box 77010
San Francisco, CA 94107

10 9 8 7 6 5 4 3 2 1
First printing, June 2024

viz.com   shonensunday.com

VOLUME 17

Ko's school trip is full of surprises as he forges connections
with old and new friends. Anko pursues a lead regarding the
truth about her father. And Mahiru and Kiku take the final
steps in their relationship as human and vampire...leaving
Ko with a lot to process.

STOP!

YOU MAY BE READING THE WRONG WAY!

READ THIS WAY

In keeping with the original Japanese comic format, this book reads from right to left—so action, sound effects, and word balloons are completely reversed to preserve the orientation of the original artwork.

Check out the diagram shown here to get the hang of things, and then turn to the other side of the book to get started!